#takedown

Written & drawn by David Blumenstein
First printed March 2015
Second printing, May 2015
Printed in Australia

Published by Pikitia Press
St Kilda West, Australia
www.pikitiapress.com
E-mail: guzumo@gmail.com

PIKITIA
PRESS

The events in this comic took place on November 6, 2014 (or in the days leading up to it).

Names and likenesses have been changed. Also, I've given everyone no hands or feet and a perfectly round head.

I tried to be fair in my storytelling, but if you're going to foam at me publicly over my bias, please do it in a way that helps my publisher sell books.

Cheers,
David Blumenstein
Brunswick, Vic.
March 2015

7:31

I was talking to the journalist over there, right, and I asked her, "You saw the **whole** video or you just saw the section?"

Hmmm.

And she was like, "I've seen the section." Right. "So what was the reaction of the girls after that?"

Hmmm.

"They left or they stayed? They stayed. So, he didn't scare them."

Hmmm.

They only see **one** view. They don't see the whole video.

People like being outraged about things. They don't want to have to look too specifically into it.

Just grabbing someone on the neck, that doesn't mean she's choking.

He was charging people 3 grand, and I thought, "Jesus, I've been on this planet a long time, I've known many people, done many things... I'd only charge you a grand!"
Ha!
CLIK CLIK CLIK
Ha ha ha
So if you want to sign up, come with me-- I'll charge you a grand and I can **guarantee** some success. How about that?
Sounds like a good proposition!
What makes you say it's **snake-oil?** Like, is that to say you've heard some sort of tale and it hasn't been as effective as it's claimed to be?

I saw her go over there -- I had no idea what she was doing...
She was great! She was very nice, and said everything I wanted to say.
The pick-up guys are all leaving... are we going to follow them or something?
We don't know if the seminar is still on.
It is.
Are you sure?
I saw a message with the location.
Really?!
It just said, "Berth 5, Southbank".
Putting it on social media!

And then some of them are maybe quiet guys, or foreign guys, who want to learn to talk to a girl.
And I kinda can't blame them, 'cause maybe that'd be me if I hadn't met Sarah.
But you wouldn't be stupid enough to follow someone like Julien.
I was a smart kid, but I still got that "Why don't girls like me they only go for pricks" shit in my head sometimes.

Mind you, I don't always agree with how the sisterhood handles this stuff, but it can be hard to say anything.

There's always a few **hard-core**, angry women who'll bite your head off if you sound like you're defending men.

But the fact is, guys don't **have** to do this shit! Like, get a fucking **hobby!** That's how **I** meet people.

Exactly. I met Sarah thru comics.

I'm not super confident, but I **seemed** confident and interesting because I was hanging out with people I liked and **making** stuff.

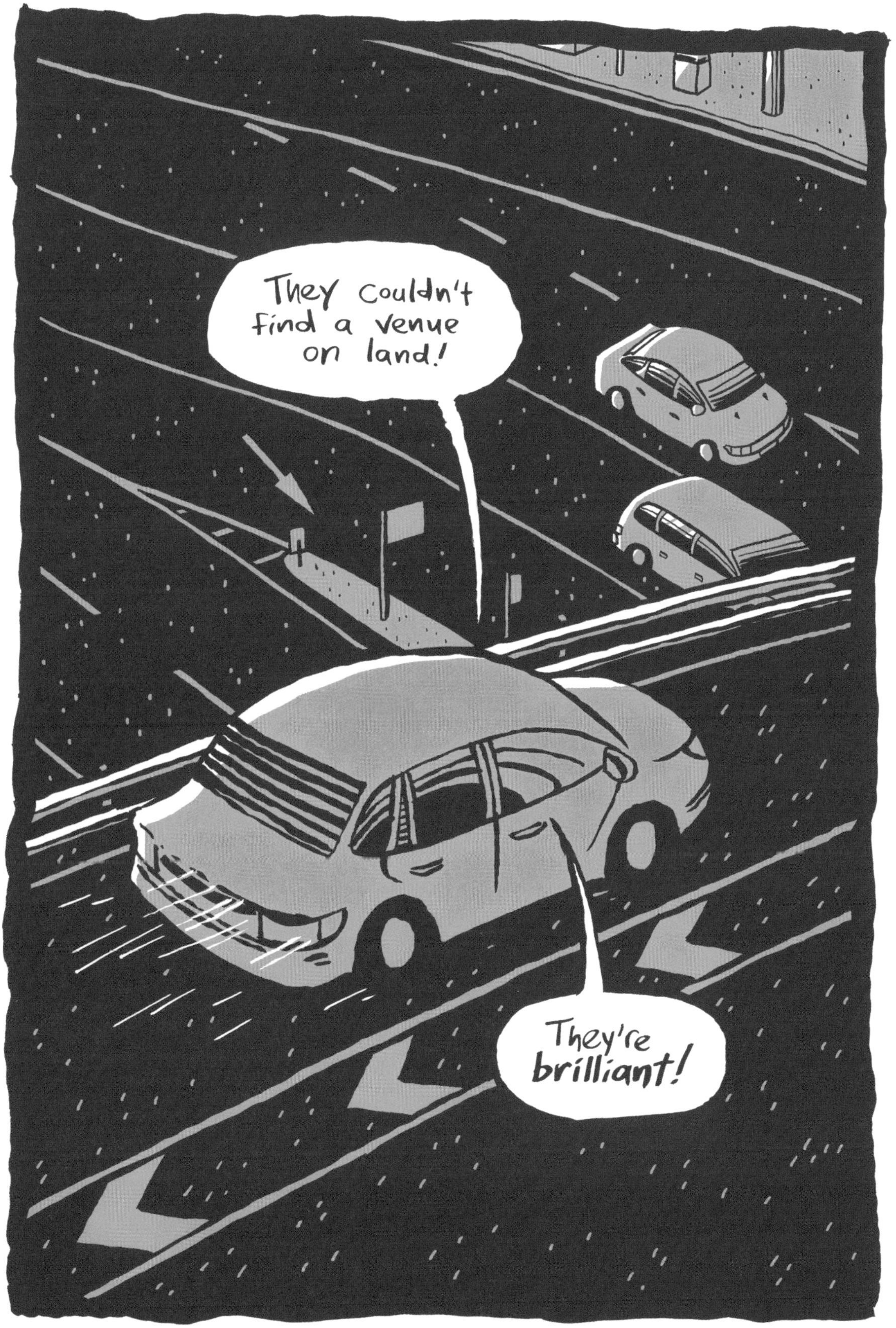
They couldn't find a venue on land!
They're **brilliant!**

9:28pm

 Damn it!
I misread the
entry about
Williamstown
and the boat
hadn't left.
looks like it's
a stand off

Fuck!

 The captain was
trying to kick
them off and
the police and
chanting and
protesters!

I MISSED FUN

 Sorry!

But I'm home
now and I've
got leftovers

 Yum

Julien never showed up to teach the seminar.

His "assistant", Max, had a go at it aboard the cruise boat, but protesters chanted and physically intervened to stop the boat leaving.

Once the boat's crew understood what was going on, they cancelled the booking. Police were called, and all the dudes were escorted back to land.

The #takedownjulienblanc campaign, sparked by one of Julien's YouTube videos ("White Male Fucks Asian Women In Tokyo (And The Beautiful Methods To It)") caused numerous seminar cancellations, and resulted in Julien's being barred from entering Australia, the U.K. and Singapore.

Julien is embarking on a World Tour starting in May 2015. He promises "effective and refined content" which will help attendees "level up".

He's skipping Japan this time.

David Blumenstein is a writer, cartoonist and animator. He's also one of the founders of Squishface Studio, an open comics studio in Brunswick, Australia. He's done comics for Crikey, Junkee, SBS comedy and Australian MAD.

Thanks

Romy Ash
Kym Bagley
Tom Doig
Matt Emery
Lisa Dempster
Chris Gooch
Justin Heazlewood
Ben Hutchings
Sarah Howell
Ben Hourigan
Natalie Pestana
Jo Waite

... and all at Squishface Studio